STRANGE FACTS OF FLIGHT

To Ann – Best wishes for a good life and good health, Have a great Summer.

Bob Kovalchik

PAGE PUBLISHING
Conneaut Lake, PA

First originally published by Page Publishing 2022

ISBN 978-1-6624-5837-8 (pbk)
ISBN 978-1-6624-5838-5 (digital)

Printed in the United States of America

To Edward Dickson,
college friend,
US Navy A-4 pilot,
KIA in Vietnam 1965.

Introduction

The author wishes the reader to visit any technical or aerospace museum to find mysteries and hidden truth that exist beyond the artifacts. This book should capture their uniqueness and virtues. Marquees found on the objects are not the total picture, nor do they reveal full information. In the case of the Wright brothers, for example, how did they get the aircraft airborne?

Obviously, there is a litany of pioneers who predated the Wrights, like George Cayley, Clement Ader, Otto Lilienthal, and others, but really, their mother taught them skills and instructed them to use household tools in Ohio and on the prairie. Susan Wright never saw the boys' flight, but their dreams came to fruition. Dr. Robert Goddard created a rocket that made a forty-one-foot ascent and led to future achievements of the Armstrongs and Gagarins in conquering the new frontier. Behind them were the von Brauns and Korolovs, who relied on legions of scientists, draftsmen and draftswomen, and test pilots to take them aloft. Still, the da Vincis and Sikorskys paved the way for vertical lift. American explorers Lewis and Clark in the nineteenth century found a newer frontier west of the Mississippi River. We now walk in their shoes and hope for success despite incredible dangers.

The ongoing struggle with many players will take us on the journey as long as funds, willpower, and an enthusiastic public provide the opportunity.

I spent twenty-seven years compiling and using these stories gleaned from books and monographs. So many aircraft crews, astronauts, veterans, and scientists made this a better and safer planet, and they also contributed. It is my fervid hope for someone who followed my tour or read the book will step on Mars or return to the moon. I had 2,087 tours of all types, so I settled with two hundred miscellaneous stories. I did not add 300 student and adult tours given at the College Park Aviation Museum in Maryland or my flying experiences at its airport. Numerous travels to Europe and US enhanced the work.

I owe a debt of gratitude to my history teachers as well and wish to thank Richard Spencer, NASA library chief, and other administrators like Rose Soldano, Amanda Ferrario, Eric Long, and Abie Hailegiorgis. Of course, my docent colleagues and a bevy of lecturers and curators over decades deserve mention.

Enjoy!

AVIATION

///

Captain Eddie Rickenbacker, American WWI pilot, got into combat in 1918 on his first sortie and mixed it up with a German. He sighted his gun from the left eye, though most used their right eye, the more dominant eye. After several passes, using up all the ammo, Eddie and the German broke away to land in their respective bases. As he got out of the cockpit of his SPAD, his mechanic noted that his leather helmet bore a streak on the left side. He commented that the round flew over the cowling and just missed him. He realized that if he had sighted with the right eye, he would have been dead. The reason he used that eye was, as a boy, he grew up near a railroad yard and steam engines gushed hot cinders. He was struck in his right eye, compromising his sight. Air service doctors did not care as the US needed combat pilots. Captain Eddie went on to shoot down twenty-six German planes and received the Medal of Honor. (E. Rickenbacker, *Rickenbacker: An Autobiography*)

World War II fighter ace Chuck Yeager downed 13 1/2 German "kills" but felt he had more. Using his P-51 gun camera, the evaluator back at his base determined another pilot shot down the same German as Yeager and awarded the two airmen one-half each. So much for the technology to evaluate tactics! (*C. Yeager, Yeager: An Autobiography*)

When the first transcontinental airmail flight took off from New York in 1920, there were few people on hand to see the event. But philatelists loaded sixteen thousand airmail covers. There was no room in the fuselage, so a suitcase was strapped on the wing and it took eighty-three hours to go to Cheyenne, Wyoming, although a regular run would take about fifty to fifty-four hours. (B. Leary, *Pilot's Directions*)

Famous woman pilot Jackie Cochran thought the Women Air Force Service gray uniform was dull, so she hired a Manhattan fashion expert and paraded two women into General Hap Arnold's and General Marshall's offices. They approved of Jackie's choice, namely Santiago blue and silver wings. (J. Cochran, *The Stars at Noon*)

The MC-202 Folgore Italian fighter plane of WWII was sent by Italian forces to help the Germans during the Russian winter of 1942. Several squadrons went from being camouflaged in desert combat to the freezing cold of the USSR, but the camouflage remained to make it a target on the ground and in the sky. Few ever returned to Italy and did little to help the Luftwaffe effort. (N. Sgarlato, *Italian Aircraft of World War II*)

It was a cool December 1909 in North Carolina when the two Wright brothers set up a launch of their "flier" on a sandy and hilly beach in Kitty Hawk. They hooked up a flywheel to the engine and got it started and flipped a coin as who would fly first. Orville won and flew into the history books as the first to fly. Wilbur flew the second and last flight fifty-nine seconds some 852 feet. That humble start created a $600-billion industry. (NASM training lecture)

Tuskegee airman Commander B. O. Davis relates in his book that his pilots never lost a bomber on their many missions. This is refuted by a B-24J pilot over Linz, Austria, who was shot down along with a Tuskegee P-51 pilot and became POWs. The Associated Press carried the story in a Washington paper a few years ago, and it was confirmed by Tuskegee historians, so the Davis information is incorrect.

However, it is a grand story about airmen like the African Americans who shepherded US bombers en route to targets in Europe. (*The Washington Post* 2008 article)

When 1930s flier Wiley Post flew around the world, he took with him $35 and returned with $34. He spent a dollar on a German souvenir. Of course, everywhere he landed he was treated like a king and paid nothing out of pocket. His fuel, servicing, and airport taxes were included when he connected with a company called Amtorg (US-Soviet), which prepaid his expenses. Amtorg was loaded with spies, and this was Stalin's way to get to USA using subterfuge. (Wiley Post, *Around the World in Eight Days*)

The author met world-famous pilot Steve Fossett in the Udvar-Hazy Museum and had a picture taken with him. I asked for his card also, but he said he was returning in a week so he would sign his photo then. He was flying to Las Vegas to meet a friend who had just purchased a Super Decathlon aircraft that he would fly. The friend allowed him to pilot it but was reported as missing. A hiker discovered the wreckage and body on a California mountain two years later. (Miscellaneous *The Washington Post* articles)

On his 1931 flight around the world, Wiley Post and navigator Harold Gatty flew eight days, fifteen hours from New York and back to set the record. On a second try in 1933, Gatty opted not to fly with Post. Why? Perhaps it was the bad habit Post had for flying until the one tank went dry. He would tap into an auxiliary tank. The *Winnie Mae* would buffet and buck and scared Gatty. This could be why Post flew alone on the same route to New York seven days, nineteen hours. (Wiley Post, *Around the World in Eight Days*)

Charles Lindbergh, on his memorable flight to Paris in 1927, took a jar that he used for his "restroom" and tossed it from the *Spirit of St. Louis*. He was asked about this by British king George V on his visit to Buckingham Palace. His flight took thirty-three hours, thirty minutes. Then he flew to London. (NASM, *Air and Space Magazine*)

A few mechanics were emplacing the J5-C Whirlwind engine into the *Spirit of St. Louis* in the shop in San Diego. A piece of the engine broke off. One mechanic remarked, "We'll fix it in no time." Lindbergh was there unnoticed, and he informed them to change the whole engine. (NASM, *Air and Space Magazine*)

Three-time aerobatics national champion Patty Wagstaff flew a German 260 Extra made with ceconite covering. Its paint scheme was the same kind for the German prestige car Porsche, which gave the aircraft high quality and appeal. (NASM training lecture by Wagstaff)

The Japanese Zero of WWII gained its name from their calendar. The type number 0 was the last digit of the Japanese year 2600 Zero-Sen. In the early years of the war, it was a king of the air, built light and fast. But as the war continued, the US Hellcat, improved Wildcat, and Corsair sent them down in flames. The Hellcat had a 19:1 kill ratio. (B. Mikesh, *Zero Fighter*)

When famed pilot and eccentric Howard Hughes got his fortune from his father's oil business, he sought to gather many WWI planes. His agents netted eighty-seven, and he put them to work making movies and more money. One was *Hell's Angels*. He liked realism and put a flier on board

who would leave when he got a signal, but the crewman did not hear the signal and died in the crash. (Howard Hughes, James Whale, and Edmund Goulding, *Hell's Angels*)

More British Hawker Hurricanes shot down Germans than its glamour cousin the Spitfire. It featured a wooden superstructure and eight machine guns. A little-known fact is its tapered cowling, which afforded the pilot an extra look at the enemy coming into view from below. One British ace saw the wing of a German, and with his fingers by the firing button, he got off a short "squirt" and shot down an ME-109. (NASM lecture on Billy Drake, *Aces High*, Christopher Shores)

Lindbergh was present at the Grumman Hellcat factory in New York and sought to fly one. The whole factory came out to see him fly twenty-five minutes. But his wheels locked and he had to try several stunts to get the wheels to come down. After three sharp pull-ups, the wheels dropped okay, much to the relief of the nervous employees and staffers. (B. Tillman, *Hellcat*)

Medal of Honor Marine pilot Joe Foss fought Japanese aircraft for sixty-three days, shot down twenty-six planes, and never had a bullet touch him. But malaria and jungle nausea did in the Pacific theater of WWII. However, it was President Roosevelt who requested him to come to the White House for his MOH ceremony and return to duty in a training unit. (Joe Foss, *Flying Marine*)

When Clarence Chamberlin piloted a Bellanca in 1927 to beat Lindbergh's long-distance flight to Paris, his copilot, and the owner of the plane, Charles Levine, asked about the oars on the plane. They were needed if they ditched into the ocean. Chamberlin told him that he forgot, and it caused the owner to fly into a frenzy! (Chamberlin, *Record Flights*)

William T. Piper bought an airplane company from another and built a factory in Bradford, Pennsylvania, only to have an accidental fire destroy it. He relocated another in Lock Haven, Pennsylvania, and created a major industry of light planes called Cubs. The FDR administration set up the CPTP Civilian Pilots Training Program as part of FDR's New Deal and took in much business, for a buyer could get one for $1,200. WWII had the government buying 5,200-plus for military operations, and they were called Grasshoppers. The aircraft (pictured below) provided scouting, moving wounded on litters, monitoring antisub activity, and shuttling staff to US bases. (D. Pisano, *To Fill the Skies With Pilots: The Civilian Pilot Training Program, 1939–46*)

An F-86 Sabrejet mechanic brought in a case of beer while stationed in Korea during the war. Korea was very hot and the beer wasn't good, so he stored it on a Sabre mission that the aircraft flew to forty thousand feet. It came back very cold, until the commanding officer found out about it. (Korean War story)

Today's expression "The whole nine yards" came from World War II, when armorers loaded the .50-caliber ammunition into the wings of P-51 Mustang fighters (shown below in Philip West's print P-51).

After WWI, there was a grand parade in Paris on Champs-Élysées. Army and Navy got front location, but pilots got the rear. An angry French pilot stole a Nieuport 17 and flew it through the famed Arc de Triomphe in protest. So much for his career in aviation!

"Wild Bill" Hopson was a seasoned airmail pilot who flew the NY-Cheyenne route. He crashed once with a one-thousand-pound package of diamonds. Only 10 percent of the mail was recovered, but not the diamonds. He wrote letters on his gloves, "W-U-V-H-R K-D-B-G-M," keying to the beacons set up for pilots in Morse code. Pilots copied letters on gloves or pasted them onto instrument panels, "When understanding very hard routes, keep directions by good methods." (Bill Leary, *Pilots' Directions*)

First flight of the flying boat Benoist XIV flew in 1914 with a passenger from St. Petersburg, Florida, to Tampa. The eighteen-mile journey landed on a river, and the passenger paid $400 for the flight. (*The Washington Star* article)

Two wrongs don't make a right, but two Wrights make an airplane. (Author's comment; useful in tours for students who appreciate funny info)

First marriage in an airplane on the ground, in a Curtiss J4 N-4, took place in 1929 as legendary flier Roscoe Turner married his sweetheart. She stood in the cockpit seat while the reverend sat on the right wing. Unfortunately, the marriage lasted only a few years and dissolved by divorce. (Turner, *Autobiography*)

A crew member cannot be color-blind and work on aircraft carriers. Many personnel are coded by their color of uniforms, viz, green for catapult work, brown for inspections, purple for fueling, red or white for radio, blue for barricades, yellow for aircraft movement. (Naval regulations)

Two pilots, Dick Merrill and Harry Richman, in 1935 flew to London to set a record over and return ASAP. Aircraft was a single-engine Vultee, which scared the pilots over the Atlantic. They emplaced forty-one thousand ping-pong balls in the wings and other spaces to hold up the plane in the event of ditching. The aircraft held up very well until it reached North America. Richman misunderstood a command from the pilot, and he dumped a large amount of fuel; this resulted in the plane to crack up in Newfoundland. The mechanics and assistants had to fix problems so it could return to New York City. The ping-pong balls were sold for $2 each, and one remains today in my hands. (J. King, *Wings of Man: Legend of Captain Dick Merrill*)

Shannon Air Museum, Fredericksburg, VA

Italian WWII pilots rarely painted their victory scores of downed aircraft because they regarded this practice as "un-Christian." Their German allies proudly marked the tail with dashes. (E. McDowell, *Flying Scoreboards*)

It was an odd situation flying in a Douglas C-47 in the Philippines during WWII, as the Japanese had the same plane, L2D Showa (only marked with red meatballs). We sold the Japanese before the war a number of the cargo planes. We referred to them as the Tabby. (R. Francillon, *Japanese Aircraft of the Pacific War*)

The Gloster E.28/39 jet flew over the Cranwell, UK, test site using the Whittle jet engine. An airman saw it and remarked, "I must be going crazy—I have just seen an aircraft without a propeller!" (J. Golley, *Whittle*)

First mass airlift in history was in 1936, when Spanish general Franco moved fourteen thousand Moroccan soldiers to Seville over the Mediterranean Sea during the Spanish Civil War. The Germans provided their cargo planes, Junkers 52, which held about fourteen seats, but as many as fifty soldiers were packed into it. (K. Ries, *Legion Condor*)

A story about a lost aircraft occurred when our secret jet, the XP-59A, disappeared in a Chicago railyard. It was transported from the factory in Buffalo to California. Security could not find it in the massive rail facility, creating a great stir. When the freight pulled out, there it was! Described by Ann Baumgartner Carl in her book. She was the first woman to fly a US jet plane. Unfortunately, the plane was too slow for WWII, and about sixty were made for training purposes only. (Ann B. Carl, *A Wasp Among Eagles*)

Austrian physicist Ernst Mach measured speed and ballistics, and his name lives on in the aerospace world. Chuck Yeager made it to Mach 1, roughly seven hundred miles per hour, in 1947 as he flew the X-1 faster than any before him. Mach, for all his beliefs, did not believe in the atomic theory. He died in 1916.

Louis XIV, the Sun King of France and great admirer of outer space, pulled off a "free agency" for space in the eighteenth century. He imported Giavanni Cassini from Italy, whereby he changed his name to Gian and stayed in France until 1712. He went blind as well and died in Paris and was buried under the floorboards now covered by concrete in a Catholic church in Paris, Left Bank, St. Jacques d'Haut Pas.

My Paris visit.

Lord Kelvin, knighted by Queen Victoria, now bears his name in science experiments regarding temperatures in units of Kelvin, but not all scientists agree with one another. Kelvin never believed that heavy aircraft or flying machines were possible. (Internet source)

Largest aircraft in the world is Ukraine's TU-225, or Mriya (Dream), sporting a 225-foot wingspan and sixteen sets of wheels. (M. Lundberg, *Century of Flight*)

Writer Maryanne Verges tells a story that when Jackie Cochran was washed out of the Hudson bomber program in Canada, her instructor lamented that she did not have enough upper-body strength in the World War II women's program. (M. Verges, *On Silver Wings*)

In Amelia Earhart's first Atlantic air crossing in 1928, she saw the passenger liner USS *America* and tried to send a message bag onto the liner's deck with oranges. Message was rolled up into the orange. Twice she tried, but the aircraft could not fly low enough to hit the target. There was no chance to land in the ocean, which had rough seas. (Amelia Earhart, *20 Hours, 40 Minutes*)

Lindbergh's flight to Paris did not have flares, but he received a $50,000 Guggenheim grant. He visited Central

American countries, equipped with two flares for landing on nonexisting airfields. The flare illuminated locations to land. Flares came from Kilgore, Texas, from Kilgore Flare Tube Co. The flags posted on his cowling are testament to his travels to open up the Caribbean area for aviation. (NASM training lecture)

Captain Eddie Rickenbacker, noted for gunning down twenty-six German aircraft in WWI, did not like the British machine guns for his SPAD; he had US-made Marlin guns, which never failed him. His secret was to hone each part with a flat stone after a flight. (Ed Rickenbacker, *Rickenbacker: An Autobiography*)

The Norden bombsight of WWII was shown off in New York's Madison Square Garden with a demostration in between a Ringling Brothers show. It featured a wooden bomb dropped into a pickle barrel. In 1942, bombardiers were ordered to destroy the bombsight if the plane was going to crash. It was such a secret that it had to be protected. After the war were fewer issues, and Engineer Norden returned to Europe. (Internet sources)

General Jimmy Doolittle's B-25 bombers needed much gasoline to get them from the USS *Hornet* to the Tokyo target. Bombers had two black-painted broom handles on the tail to ward off any Japanese fighters so extra gas cans could be carried in lieu of ammunition. (J. Doolittle,

I Could Never Be So Lucky Again)

A Tuskegee pilot was on a strafing run over a German airport, low approach. After he returned to base, his mechanic found a German's scalp in the air vent of a P-51 fighter. Proof of the old adage "War is hell." (NASM lecture)

A Curtiss Jenny No. 4983, now in the Udvar-Hazy Museum and used in New England for training purposes, bears an animal of unknown identity. That squadron selected the animal for use on the plane but left no records to show what it is. It is lost to history.

Admiral Noel Gaylor was a WWII fighter pilot who was selected to fly a captured Japanese Zero to a naval base outside Washington, DC. Pilots were to evaluate the plane and note its character. Gaylor was fearful that antiaircraft gunners protecting government buildings might take pot-shots at this enemy aircraft. He has the notoriety of flying the only enemy plane over the US capital in wartime. (NASM lecture by Noel Gaylor)

Lockheed F-104 Starfighter was a 1950s Mach 2 fighter, but it had a serious flaw at low takeoff. If a pilot had to eject from a flameout, it was fatal. African American Robert Lawrence died when his parachute failed, and he could have been the first one to go into space for his race. (M. Cassutt, *Who's Who in Space*)

SPACE

Kathy Sullivan was the first US woman to walk in space in 1984 while an astronaut on STS-41G. Just in 2020, she went to the deepest part of the Pacific Ocean, in the Mariana Trench, 35,800 feet. No other astronaut has achieved such height and depth. (*The Washington Post* article)

Russian cosmonaut Yuri Gagarin was the world's first space person with his Vostok 1961 flight. He uttered the first word there also, *payekali*, which means "Let's go." Gagarin did not complete his turn but was short. He left Vostok at fifteen thousand feet in a cylinder, then activated a manual lever to send him via parachute to a small village named Smelovka. He was picked up by a military helicopter and became world-famous. These items are seen in the picture to the right and found in a Russian museum in Moscow called Cosmonautics. This information was made public in 1987, but the secrecy was created by USSR as the Federation Aeronautic International rule requires all spacefarers to return in the same vehicle. (G. Hooper, *The Soviet Cosmonaut Team*)

NASM's touchable moon rock weighs twenty-eight grams, is volcanic basalt, and is smooth from the faithful touching, and on the Washington Mall, there are moon rocks in glass cases in the Smithsonian National Museum of Natural History. However, those are not touchable. (NASM info).

The first Black in space is often confused with the first African American. Cuban Arnaldo Tamayo-Mendez flew on Russian T-38 for seven days in 1980, while Guy Bluford flew on a shuttle, STS-8, in 1984. Bluford went on to fly on three more shuttle flights, while the Cuban never got back to space. (J. Burgess, *Intercosmos*)

Curiosity, a major Mars rover, had a 1909 VDB rare penny superglued on its front support to calibrate its many cameras. It has a grainy effect from its exposure to Martian atmosphere. VDB are initials of Victor D. Brenner, the US mintmaster. Coin in uncirculated condition is worth $100-plus. (NASA information)

Can you drive a car on the moon? Yes, if it is electric. If not, there is no oxygen that can use the gasoline to power the car. A spark is essential to ignite the fuel. (J. Irwin, *To*

Rule the Night)

First African American woman astronaut in space is Mae Jemison, whose mother wanted her to be a dancer. She was afraid of high places, but she flew on STS-47 in 1992 some two hundred miles high. (M. Jemison bio)

I spent five summers in USSR during the Cold War and always visited VDNH in Moscow (Economic Achievement Pavilion), an open-air museum called Cosmos on each of its sides. Birds came in and deposited their "doo" on the spacecraft. Hardly a good way to have a space museum. (Personal experience)

Astronaut Alan B. Shepard, on Apollo 14, sneaked a golf six iron on his capsule, intent on hitting a golf ball on the moon. He did so but missed first stroke. His second try, he claimed that went far away. Another astronaut contemporary told me it did not travel so far. The six iron now is in the PGA museum in New Jersey. (A. Shepard, *Moonshot*)

Yuri Gagarin, the Russian who flew first to space in 1961, was bussed to his launch tower. He needed to relieve himself, so he got out of the bus and urinated on a tire. This started a tradition that cosmonauts using Russian launches do, but women choose to urinate in a cup and pour it on a tire. US and foreign spacemen and spacewomen also do so. (Roscosmos, Russian space agency)

Is there money on the moon? Yes, no dollars or coins, but diamonds and plenty of helium-3 isotopes scattered via solar winds. The H3I a ton would be the equivalent of hundreds of years of coal use, according to moonwalker Harrison Schmitt's book *Return to the Moon*.

Space community and the public have implored Congress and presidents for more funds, and NASA contends its argument is, "No bucks, no Buck Rogers." (NASA information)

When the fender broke off on the Lunar Roving Vehicle Apollo 17, NASA stated under the seats were map folders and duct tape; astronauts Cernan and Schmitt took care of the issue. It was captured on canvass by astronaut artist Al Bean.

I was traveling in San Francisco in July 1969 when Apollo 11 landed on the moon. There was a rush to get early *San Francisco Chronicle* with the red headline "Men on the Moon." Fools exist, too, as a Berkeley tabloid showed one astronaut photo and the paper exclaimed, "So What?"

Astrophysicist Clyde Tombaugh is credited with the discovery of planet Pluto in 1931 and has henceforth been its defender. But twenty scientists met in the International Astronautics Union Prague convention to downplay it as a dwarf planet. Tombaugh also denounced the big bang theory. (Letter from Tombaugh, 1996)

Eighth planet from the sun, Neptune, was submitted to the International Astronautics Union by English astronomer John Adams in 1846. But his paperwork was late and a Frenchman, Le Verrier, received credit. (NASA information)

The Iridium company created sixty-six relay satellites circling the globe for fast communication. But their receiver was like a brick, weighed a pound, and did not work inside skyscrapers. Company went bankrupt in 2002 and was faced with great competition. (*Satellite Magazine* 2002)

Astronaut and moonwalker Jim Irwin said he felt like a baby because he needed help to get into the Lunar Roving Vehicle. Irwin, with his very small five-foot-seven thin build, could not reach the seat belts. David Scott, Apollo 15 commander, tucked him each time they stopped. (J. Irwin, *To Rule the Night*)

Owner Paul Allen's SpaceShipOne was the first privately built spacecraft that was carried to forty-six thousand feet on the *White Knight*, then launched with Mike Melville to one hundred kilometers (sixty-two miles) space boundary. Melville employed ping-pong balls, which floated, to mark his space location. He opened a pocket to release candy, which also floated to confirm space. He and Brian Binnie, who also flew SpaceShipOne, claimed a $10,000 Ansari X Prize. (A. Ansari, *My Dream of Stars*)

Mercury space suits were made by the B. F. Goodrich Company with a large slash zipper in the front, but astronauts complained that much money was spent on the protective suit in space and in the hands of a little old seamstress specialist. If the zipper stuck, astronauts would be in big trouble. (A. Shepard, *Moon Shot*)

Japanese cosmonaut Toyahiro Akiyama spent seven days in space, the first of his countrymen, on TM-10. Tokyo Broadcasting Company paid $12,000 for his ride to the Soviets. He had several foibles—namely, he smoked four packs of cigarettes daily (you cannot smoke in space) and lacked more clothing for the duration. (Sotheby's New York sale catalog 1993; M. Cassutt, *Who's Who in Space*)

Before Gagarin made his historic space trip, the Russians sent a mannequin in 1961 with parachute to test its feasibility. It landed in the Ural Mountains, USSR. Citizens reported it found, and a military unit was dispatched to protect it from tampering. Villagers surrounded the soldiers and argued that the cosmonaut needed medical attention; never did they know that the parachutist was not human. This is accounted in the Sotheby's catalog of USSR 6516, nicknamed Ivan Ivanovich, and sold for $190,000. (Sotheby's New York catalog sale 1993)

When Soviet cosmonaut Sergei Krikalev returned from space in 1992 after 312 days, he was no longer a citizen of the USSR, as a new nation had emerged, that of the Russian Federation. (www.spacefacts.de)

US astronaut Ed White had trouble closing the hatch in space for Gemini 4. He had the distinction of being the first American to venture into space for twenty-two minutes. Commander Jim McDivitt opted to return to Earth and not try another EVA in 1965. (M. Cassutt, *Who's Who in Space*)

President Trump called for the Space Command in 2019, but a new name came forth, Guardian, and Mike Hopkins was the first Guardian and is a colonel in the Air Force and hails from Missouri. He was captain of the University of Illinois 1991 football team. (*The Washington Times*)

Mercury MR-4, launched in 1961 with Gus Grissom, flooded in the ocean and carried a roll of Mercury dimes. The spacecraft was recovered from its watery grave in 1992. Coins were shared with the Kansas Cosmodrome and other museums, though some may be in private hands. (Network News)

Kathy Sullivan, first US woman to walk in space, thought to herself over Boston, *There are a lot of Sullivans down there.* She was busy working on an antenna for SIR-B, refueling hydrazine for the satellite, and taking photos of her efforts. (H. Cooper, *Before Lift-Off*)

Dental work in space was necessary at times, but equipment is lacking. One notable case was on a Russian Mir station, when a cosmonaut, Vasily Tsibliev, cracked a tooth. A painkiller was used until he returned to Earth.

Indonesia had a cosmonaut dentist, but he worked on an engineering project. (J. Linenger, *Off the Planet*)

Just before the launch of Russian Sputnik in 1957, chief designer Sergei Korolev lectured his compatriots about the spacecraft. He put a velvet covering under it and concluded that people the world over would hail the craft as the first Earth satellite. (J. Harford, *Korolev*)

What happens to women astronauts' hair in space? It tends to pull upward, as seen in astronaut Catherine "Cady" Coleman Shuttle Flight Columbia STS-73's photo.

President Nixon authorized 135 countries in the United Nations to receive a sliver of moon rocks, which are displayed in countries' museums, but some have been stolen, lost, or unaccounted for. In all, we have 842 pounds of moon rocks from the Apollo mission in the sixties to seventies period. The NASM rock measures twenty-eight grams, or one ounce. (Internet sources)

Hubble Space Telescope instruments can detect ten

times as sharp as those that can detect four hundred miles because they are not distorted by Earth's atmosphere or shaken from disturbances. This was why Hubble was carried to space on STS-31 shuttle and has been at L2 since 1993. (NASA.gov)

When astronauts on the moon brought the moon rocks into the LEM, they depressurized and sense of smell took over. It smelled like burnt ashes. The rocks were deposited into a special case created by Union Carbide and hermetically sealed for return to Earth. (B. Aldrin, *Men on the Moon*)

STS-41B—in 1984, Challenger number designation changed with this flight: (4) year of flight; second digit, launch site, Florida; (B) second launch of the year. (M. Cassutt, *Who's Who in Space*)

How did astronaut Mae Jemison get a D in girls PE (1969)? She was slow to polish her shoes. Not a slob, but not as clean as her teacher, and she did not sew her name on her gym outfit as fast as she was ordered. She did get on board STS-47 in 1992. Story comes from her biography, *Find Where the Wind Goes.*

First mother in space was Dr. Anna Fisher, who had a baby girl, ten pounds, before she flew on board shuttle STS-51A Discovery in 1984. She handled the Remote Manipulator Arm while on the eight-day flight. (M. Cassutt, *Who's Who in Space*)

We know that the Russians sent dogs into space, like

Laika, but did the US use cats or dogs or spiders? Yes, on Skylab, there were two spiders, Anita and Arabella. One died in space, the other on the ground. (J. Carr, *Around the World in 84 Days*)

A satellite is a human-made, free-flying object that creates data on weather, the military, environment, directions, and communication, like the Telstar in 1960s, which could bring locations from anywhere. (D. J. Baker, *Planet Earth*)

Kate Rubins, astronaut from California, has been working on rare data like DNA in space. She has a PhD in science and came from the Ashcan 9 training class. She totaled three hundred days in space on two International Space Station flights. (www.spacefacts.de)

David Scott promised the Air Force cadets he would bring back a falcon feather on his Apollo 15 mission after he tried the Galileo experiment, as the moon is airless. This featured a hammer in one hand and feather on another. Falcon is the mascot of the cadets. On his flight in 1971, he made two attempts but could not find the elusive feather. Probably hidden in the moondust. After his return to Earth, he apologized to them. Another moonwalker, Al Bean, painted the scene. (A. Bean, *Lithograph*)

Iranian American Anousheh Ansari brought up meat-loaf to the International Space Station and tried to give it to another one but had to push it as it was much like Starship *Enterprise*. (A. Ansari, *My Dream of Stars*)

Sally Ride's book *Mystery of Mars* alludes to water disappearing from its surface since it is trapped in rocks like a sponge. (S. Ride, *Mystery of Mars*)

 Moonwalker David Scott on Apollo 15 wore three watches. First was the official one given by NASA, created by Omega, second one timed with New York, and recently, a third attributed to him connected with projects he worked on the moon. This one worn when he saluted the flag, took photos, and performed the Galileo experiment. The third

one, a Bulova, placed in an auction, netted $1.6M from description "RR Auction Item 9001).

Perseverance is exploring Mars surface to bring Mars sample rocks back to Earth. (www.nasa.gov)

Mars weather is normally very cold but can be eighty degrees plus at its torrid zone during its summer. It also features weird situations, like dust devils rising to twenty miles. It also has one-third [the] gravity that of Earth. NASA, *StarDate: Guide to the Solar System*)

The USSR had their own spy satellite system in space. They used photos from an MKF-6M camera, then sent them earthbound with an ablative bucket to be secured by helicopter, but it had flaws and were able to get selective data from NATO exercises and special military locations only. (C. Burgess, *Interkosmos*)

A new power, that of solar electric ion propulsion, gave the *Dawn* spacecraft effort to reach Vesta and Ceres, two of the biggest asteroids in 2011–2012. Investigations measured their characteristics. These two distant locations are between planets Neptune and Jupiter.

What is the nearest planet? you ask. Mercury, Mars. No. You are standing on it—Earth!

When I served in the military, we were shaving in the morning and question came up about a sun probe the US had sent into space. I asked one soldier, "How do we save it from burning up?" He responded, "Why don't they go at night?" (Commentary)

Thousands of small and large planets, called exoplanets, have been discovered with Hubble and other telescopes as well as TESS (Transiting Exoplanet Survey Satellite).

Launched 2017, it has opened more windows into deep space and created a legion of enthusiasts who hope to find life somewhere.

The first exoplanet found in 1995 was the 51 Pegasi by Didier Queloz and Michael Mayer. Many more have been discovered well into the thousands, with names like 70 Virginis and 55 Cancri. (NASA information)

The Viking landers, which made it to Mars in 1976, returned 3,542 images on number 1 and sent 3,043 on number 2 and were 4,600 miles from each other. An oddity is that the first one had battery problems, and the second one was launched first. (A. Siddiqi, *Beyond Earth*)

The heliopause is the demarcation of where interstellar space begins and the end of the sun's influence. It is a termination shock, and solar winds slow to zero. NASA's IBEX was launched in 2008 but did not travel nine billion miles although it detected particles.

Dragon spacecraft, or Falcon 9 SpaceX, operates from Kennedy Space Center, Florida. This is Elon Musk's company, and the vehicle can carry crew and cargo. Cargo with 1,150 pounds can return with 1,500 pounds of junk and material. (Internet sources)

In May 2020, two astronauts ventured to link with the International Space Station by way of Elon Musk's SpaceX Dragon and returned to Earth in the Gulf of Mexico. The pair were Commander Doug Hurley and Bob Behnken, and they were a vindication of NASA partnership with private industry. (Internet sources)

US trips to the moon were facilitated by a computer nicknamed DSKY, with thirty-eight thousand words and 17.5-pound weight and eight-by-eight-by-seven-inch size and shared by two astronauts on the Lunar Module and Command Module. There was a spare also in each module according to R and R auctions.

Astronaut Jack Swigart replaced Mattingly, who might have had measles, on Apollo 13. About 150 miles up, he notified IRS on April 15 he had not filed income tax. IRS gave him the longest extension in history to file the tax. (J. Lovell, *Lost Moon*)

Many fellow aviation astronauts were skeptical of Harrison Schmitt since he was not a pilot. Previous ones were. Schmitt learned to fly a Cessna 172 and got a license. He showed them! (M. Collins, *Liftoff*)

US Skylab space station set a record of eighty-four days in space with Commander Jerry Carr. But the men had to eat granola bars for sixteen days since lockers had no spare food. NASA did not look good on this situation and did not admit it. Carr's book *Around the World in 84 Days* told the real story!

Moonwalker Charlie Duke, Apollo 16, had a souvenir photo of his family, and as he drove on the LRV, he tossed it onto the moon's surface. Perhaps someone will find it in the future, unless moondust obscures it. The astronauts could carry some articles in a PPK (personal preference kit), pictures, four-leaf clovers, religious articles, pins, and other items, for lunar memorabilia. (C. Duke, *Moonwalker*)

When cosmonaut Alexei Leonov did his Voskhod 1 walk in space, his entry required him to squeeze through a tube for ten minutes. He saw an amazing sight of the Earth that no human had ever seen. He tried a return but had his space suit ballooned. He depressurized some but came into the spacecraft. He was reproached by Russian Mission Control. (A. Leonov, *Two Sides of the Moon*)

Apollo 11 astronaut Buzz Aldrin noticed a broken circuit breaker switch for the ascent engine. The Lunar Module was stuck on the moon. Buzz used his Fisher pen to poke into the opening and activate the switch. Fisher pens have been used by NASA since Apollo 7 and are made in Boulder City, Nevada. They write underwater, on ceilings, in space and are antigravity and, of course, saved Apollo LEM. (Internet sources)

The GOES-R satellite (Geostationary Operational Environmental Satellite) will serve our weather reporting and environmental studies for the near future. There are two that patrol our skies and oceans: 15 GOES is West Coast and Pacific Ocean, 13 East USA. The R will cover US for ten years' life span with much more attention to hurricanes, weather, and environment from 22,500 miles in space. This is called Clarke Orbit, named after Sir Arthur Clarke, who began GEO idea. (A. Clarke, *Exploration of Space*)

It is hoped that a new Webb Telescope, to be launched on a French Ariane 5 rocket, will be able to look out to the beginning of time, 13.5 billion years. It has a 6.5-meter lens, while Hubble had 2.4 meters. There are four main devices. It is launched from Guyana, and its space location is L-2 (Lagrange point). (NASA information)

Artist's View of M60-UCD1 Black Hole

Vera Rubin (1928–2016) was a Washington, DC, native and Georgetown graduate with much knowledge of deep space. She discovered the black holes, of which science knows little. They are an anomaly of space, sucking bodies like exoplanets and planets to unknown sites. (Internet sources)

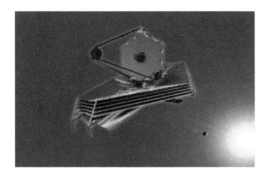

Only three space shuttles exist in museums today. *Discovery* is in the Udvar-Hazy Museum in Chantilly, Virginia; *Atlantis* in Houston; and *Endeavor* in Los Angeles. Two were destroyed in accidents, *Columbia* in 2003, and *Challenger* in 1986. The ones in museums are not open for touring. (NASA information)

Grigori G. Nelyubov was Gagarin's backup cosmonaut for the first man in space, but his rising star fell quickly when he opposed his superiors in 1961. He was dismissed and sent to Soviet Far East. He was drunk, fell from a bridge, and killed by a train in 1966. (G. Hooper, *The Soviet Cosmonaut Team*)

The International Space Station took thirteen years to build, with the backing of the USA, Russians, Japanese, and European Space Agency in operation and crewed since

2000. Currently planned to go to 2024. Some seventeen nations have put it in place, and many countries have sent crews. Science and understanding about low Earth orbit has taken place, and now commercial operations have begun. (NASA information)

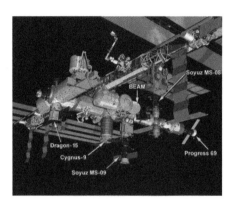

The first two Soviet cosmonauts chosen to fly to the moon were Alexei Leonov and Oleg Makarov, but there were too many engines on the first stage (thirty-three) of the N-1 rocket. The way it would be canceled if one engine malfunctioned was, the whole stage would disintegrate. Four attempts were made without crew, and they all blew up—in 1969, 1971, and two in 1972. This ended the manned Russian moon program, and they switched to the idea of a space station. (W. Matson, *Cosmonautics: Colorful History*)

Werner von Braun was the genius of the US moon program and was fortunate to be captured by US Forty-Fourth Army at the end of WWII. He and 126 scientists came to America and built the Apollo program, which culminated in six trips to the moon. The Germans avoided capture by Russians and knew they would get better treatment and reception from the USA. (M. Neufeld, Wernher von Braun biography)

Scott Kelly, veteran astronaut, flew on the International Space Station on his phenomenal flight for 348 consecutive days to set the American record. He performed numerous science projects and created information to compare with his twin brother and fellow spaceman, Russian Kornienko. (NASA information)

First African American to fly on Space vehicle X is Victor Glover, naval officer and VF-18 pilot. He performed a spacewalk to change its batteries and spent 167 days in space. (www.spacefacts.de)

The major human problems with space are a loss of bone density (1 percent a month), eye problems, and skeletal damage called osteopenia. Kelly program went from 2015 to 2016. So far, no progress revealed to correct the problems, though NASA is working diligently. (National Institutes of Health)

No one is expecting astronauts to visit planet Venus, not with a surface heat of nine hundred degrees and an atmosphere which pressure is ninety times that of Earth. Carbon dioxide also is a killer as a poison. Thick clouds also obscure its surface, which probably feature volcanic activity. (NASA fact sheet, www.nasa.gov)

The attention is on Mars, which US has sent rovers and satellites to to observe as much as possible. Robotic Maven sent in 2013 showed a stream of particles from the sun that eliminated the magnetic field. Once it had a magnetic field, but four billion years later, its molten core froze. It will pose many problems if we land with people and hope to colonize. (NASA report)

Smallest planet is Mercury and closest to the sun. Its diameter is three thousand miles, and it was photographed by *Mariner 10* in 1974. It has craters named after Margaret Mead, painters like Dali, and writers like Edgar Allan Poe. It was visited by the probe *Messenger* and has a hot climate, but in evening, temperatures can drop very low. (Internet sources)

The *Progress* freighter from Russia is a resupply vehicle to bring water, propellant, and gas to the International Space Station along with SpaceX Dragon. It can boost the ISS to higher level and can work autonomously or operated by crew. After unloading, it can be filled with trash and returned to be burned up. (T. Furniss, *Space Vehicles*)

One day at the US Naval Academy, a conversation with our five hundredth astronaut, Chris Cassidy, told a story that there was a problem with equipment failure. There was no available handbook on the ISS. One of the Russian cosmonauts secured a hammer and hit the device hard. Suddenly, it worked! Moral of the story is, one needs to know how to improvise. (NASA astronaut C. Cassidy)

The *Gemini 4* spacecraft produced the first US EVA (extravehicular activity), or spacewalk. Ed White, a DC high school product, spent twenty-two minutes outside the craft. But in training, the crew had difficulty to close the hatch. In space it proved similarly, so Commander Jim McDivitt and NASA Control decided to return to Earth and not try another spacewalk. (M. Collins, *Liftoff*)

I recall after watching the arrival of Apollo 11 on the moon, I took a cab in San Francisco to go to a restaurant. The cabdriver reflected that this was not correct and the government created a base in the Pacific somewhere to hoodwink the US TV networks. Cabdrivers know it all? (Personal)

Our Pershing II missile got its name via General Medaris, a World War I veteran. Naming rights were too current, and no one WWI existed, so Medaris put Pershing's top commander's name on the missile. It was deployed in Europe with a range of 1,200 miles and was deadly accurate in 1983. (Defense Department information)

Gürragchaa, the Mongolian cosmonaut who flew in 1981, came back to a hero's welcome, but it wore off when his nation threw off communism. He found his capsule was taken from a museum in Mongolia and put in some storage for a mall. He then put the spacecraft into a new room in his house built to accommodate it. Now it is back in a new space museum in Ulan Bator, the capital city. (C. Burgess, *Interkosmos*)

First Soviet rocket was launched in 1933 in Nakhabino, outside Moscow, and built by top scientist Mikhail Tikonravov. It flew to 1,300 feet with the GIRD 09 team-work's help. (A. Siddiqi, *Challenge to Apollo*)

The Parker Solar Probe, launched in 2018, will get to about three million miles from the sun and select information from its surface. Dr. Eugene Parker, age ninety-two, was actually on hand to see the liftoff in Florida, and it was the first time a named person was there to view a launch. (nasa.gov/jhuapl.edu)

The first untethered spacewalk took place from the *Challenger* shuttle by Bruce McCandless. The movement in February 1984 went 320 feet, and a six-hour EVA ensued with Robert Stewart also. Later in 1994, astronaut Mark Lee tested a SAFER backpack from the shuttle *Discovery*. The small self-contained device uses twenty-four fixed-position thrusters to expel nitrogas to move in a rescue assist. (NASA lithographs)

Soviet's Anatoly Solovyev owns the greatest amount of time in spacewalking as he flew five flights with 82.22 days EVA in space before retiring in 2003. His time frame was 1988–1997. The US leader is Mike Lopez-Alegria with 67 days EVA. (www.spacefacts.de)

Dr. Ellen Ochoa, first Latin American woman in space, flew four shuttle missions with forty days accumulated, then became a director of one of the NASA sites.

Dr. Peggy Whitson is the top US flier in space with 665 days on a variety of missions to the International Space Station, shuttle missions, including some EVAs on NASA projects. (www.spacefacts.de)

Russians tried use of a lander fully automatic, called Luna (Moon) 16, in 1970, and it was a success, which brought back 101 grams of lunar soil, similar to US Apollo 12. Soil samples were shared with science people in countries of East Germany, Iraq, and France. (A. Siddiqi, *Beyond Earth*)

President Nixon was unable to meet the Apollo 11 astronauts after they returned from the moon because of a quarantine. The early moon flights were subject to intense concern because of contaminants. The book and movie

Andromeda Strain alarmed the USA. This stopped with Apollo 15–17 flights. (T. Benford, *Space Program Quiz and Fact Book*)

Voyager 1 carried a golden record with fifty-five greetings in different languages, sounds of world songs, photos of world scenes (black-and-white), music of Mozart, Bach, and US pop singer Chuck Berry. US president Jimmy Carter and UN figure Kurt Waldheim were also heard to extend a welcome to a UFO. (A. Siddiqi, *Beyond Earth*)

Voyager 2 went farther in distance and transmitted images of the Jovian moons like Callisto, Ganymede, Europa, Io, and Amalthea beyond Earth. The craft also found wind speeds of Uranus's atmosphere marked at 724 kilometers per hour and secured five of Uranus's moons with rare photos. It also flew past Neptune, checking its winds at 1,100 kilometers per hour. (A. Siddiqi, *Beyond Earth*)

The satellite *Clementine*, built in Washington, DC, got to the moon and photographed 1.6 million images mostly one hundred meters from its surface. The Titan

II rocket launched from Vandenberg AFB in 1994 and was so-named from the song that it was not coming back and burned up in August 1994. (A. Siddiqi, *Beyond Earth*)

Apollo 8 was the first flight that broke Earth's atmosphere and journeyed to the moon as a test effort by NASA in 1968. First Saturn rocket piloted by humans. Commander Borman Jim Lovell and Bill Anders were on the six-day mission. It is loaded on board the USS *Yorktown*. (J. Lovell, *Lost Moon*)

Measurement in space can be tricky, and Gian Cassini, Italian astronomer, in 1672 felt that the Earth was about eighty-seven million miles from the sun; actually today, we believe it is ninety-three million. He used a parallax method. Stick your arm out with thumb up and cover your left eye, then cover your right eye. (A. Siddiqi, *Beyond Earth*)

Gian Domenico Cassini, 1625 - 1712. Italian astronomer.

There is considerable interest to privatize space. New vehicles are being worked on, like SpaceX, Boeing Starliner, Blue Origin, Sierra Nevada, Virgin Galactic, and may dominate the future if successful. All are products of billionaires, investors, and space enthusiasts and what have you. (Articles from *SpaceNews*, 2020)

Astronauts had constraints of their size if they flew in space. One could not be taller than 6-4 nor smaller than 4-11. Suits made in Delaware required such matters owing to cost. James van Hoften was six foot four and made two shuttle flights and did two satellite services on EVA work. He earned a PhD in hydraulic engineering and flew sixty missions in the Vietnam War according to Mike Cassutt's *Who's Who in Space*.

Katherine Johnson, NASA math scientist, helped astronauts like John Glenn get to space but never got proper recognition. Now a movie exists, a Barbie doll, and a resupply rocket. Cygnus will fly in her honor with her name. (NASA Public Relations Office)

A stainless steel plaque designed by NASA tech services' Jack Kinzler is on the moon, fourth rung of the ladder, from the Apollo 11 flight. Others were put on the LEM and ladders, but the Apollo 13 plaque is in the hands of Jim Lovell, who never got to the moon. (J. Lovell, *Lost Moon*)

Chinese Tianwen and United Arab Emirates have created Mars vehicles and will investigate the planet along with the American rovers and satellites, including India's interest. (www.MarsDaily.com)

First US satellite launched in 1958, Explorer 1, spotted the Van Allen Belts, which are highly charged electrons and protons, six hundred miles to three thousand miles, and nine to fifteen thousand miles beyond Earth. The satellite had nickel cadmium batteries, and they lasted much longer than those of the first satellite (Sputnik), twelve years in space. (T. Furniss, *Space Vehicles*)

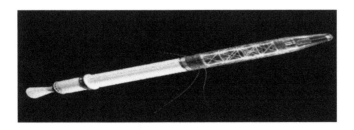

The Corona Project, a spy satellite built by Lockheed-Martin with the cooperation of the CIA and Air Force, patrolled over the USSR, PRC, and Iran to protect US interests. It led to improved versions, like the Key Holes 7-14, and had a one-and-a-half-meter resolution. Film buckets were captured by various aircraft, like the Fairchild C-119 Packet and C-130. (D. Brugioni, *Eyeball to Eyeball: The Cuban Missile Crisis*, "Aircraft")

AVIATION

Aircraft licenses with low numbers were highly prized, as Howard Hughes got number 80. Oddly, the Wright brothers did not get 1–2, but Bill McCracken from Civil Aviation Board was number 1. Planes from USA had letter *N* from 1926 to present; others, like UK, had G, Germany D, France F, etc. Ours from Navy administrators and deference to the NC-4 flying boat that crossed the Atlantic. (NASM story)

Lindbergh flew to Paris in 1927, but he did not receive the prestigious Collier Trophy. Charles Lawrance, who built his air-cooled engine, J-5C, received the trophy. (NASM, *Paper Airplane* newsletter)

The F-100 US jet was not the fastest but the last plane capable of delivering the atomic bomb by a single person. It flew on Misty, secretive missions, in Vietnam. Now long retired. (R. Hallion, *Test Pilots*)

Warren Grimes created an aviation company with red, green, and white lights to service aircraft and make the industry safer in the 1930s. He is in the Aviation Hall of Fame in Dayton, Ohio, and his company has been taken over by Honeywell Corp. (Internet sources)

The Key brothers, Fred and Al, flew over Meridian, Mississippi, in 1935 in a Curtiss Robin to set a record for twenty-seven straight days. Some ten thousand fans milled around to watch the event. Gas lines were sent down from a trailing aircraft to fill the Robin's tank. The engine noise was so deafening they wrote notes to each other. There was gas spilled, and they had to make engine adjustments for the *Old Miss*. (S. Owens, *Flying Key Brothers*)

Aircraft pitot tube refers to measuring air pressure that leads to airspeed. A French engineer, Henri Pitot, working in the eighteenth century, has given rise to our present day. (My article, NASM newsletter)

Duralumin is a metal combination of aluminum, copper, and manganese that, when stretched out, can be used in aircraft to make it more durable and enjoy a longer life span. It can be traced to WWI, when a German builder, Alfred Wiln, created the Junkers J4 in 1918. Many international aircraft makers employed the material. (Internet facts)

Fred Weick (1899–1993) was a pilot, air designer, and engineer who created civilian aircraft like the Ercoupe,

Pawnee, and Piper Cherokee, wrote a book on propellers, and was renowned for the NACA cowling. He was an expert on aircraft safety. (Internet facts and R. Hallion's *Test Pilot*)

A 1941 test of the Gloster 28/39 British jet plane flew about, and a RAF airman asked, "Frank, it flew?" Whittle responded, "That's what it damned well was supposed to do." Today, it hangs in the London Science Museum, on the third floor. (J. Golley, *Whittle*)

The V-1 German pulse jet was also carried with a special-purpose two-engine HE-111 stamped EC-8 near the support jet. When the crew got into the aircraft, German staff did not trust enlisted men with firing operations. Only pilot and armorer had details to fire. Thus, a curtain hid the V-1 so the EM could not see it. The Nazis felt that if captured, the enlisted men would reveal information. (Museum of Flight in Seattle newsletter)

On Steve Fossett's balloon flight around the world, *Spirit of Bud Light*, which left Northam, Australia, on June 18, 2002, he carried a six-pack of beer. He did not drink any during the fourteen-day journey. It was for the benefactors. (*The Washington Post* news articles)

German 262 jet crew had fingers and hands severed by placing them into the nozzle intakes. They had to place screens in front when the jet was warming up. (*The Washington Post* news articles)

Roland Garros, a French WWI ace, was downed in German territory. His plane had machine guns firing through the propeller, novel for its time. Tony Fokker, a Dutchman working for the Germans, seized on the idea and had guns working in forty-eight hours according to his biography, and that gave them the advantage in 1917. (A. Fokker, *Flying Dutchman*)

The US fighter P-39 Airacobra had a big cannon firing through the cockpit and near the Alison engine, but it was a weak plane in the Pacific theater as it had poor performance. We shipped 1,500 assorted aircraft to the Russians in the Lend-Lease Program in WWII. Soviets loved its cannon, and one of their aces, Alexander Pokryshkin, shot down fifty-nine Germans and knocked out their tanks, which were lightly armored on the top. (H. Siedl, *Stalin's Eagles*)

Sir Frank Whittle patented the first jet engine in 1931

and saw the plane 28/39 fly at Cranwell, UK, in 1941. German designer Hans von Ohain had a jet going in 1938, but neither men had met until the Second World War was well over in 1966. No information about what was said.

First African American combat pilot, Eugene Bullard, flew French Nieuport 17s later in WWI. He had been a foot soldier from Georgia who fled USA on a ship. He landed in France, only to face German invasion, and enlisted in the French Foreign Legion. Later, he was wounded but wished to fly an aircraft. (P. Carisella, *Black Swallows of Death*)

A model of the aircraft carrier US *Enterprise* exists and a story was told that two Navy vets met in a café and exchanged sea tales. Both were on the same ship at the same time but had never met the other during their lengthy sea duty. The carrier held five thousand personnel. (Sailor story, Navy sea story)

Wiley Post's Vega, flown in 1931, had an electronic sensor that notified him of ice on the wings. If excessive, he could fly lower to warmer air. Excellent information for a flier going around the world. (W. Post, *Around the World in 8 Days*)

Wiley Post flew to fifty thousand feet and encountered the intensity of the jet stream. He used a crude diving suit that is preserved in the Udvar-Hazy Museum by NASM. (W. Post, *Around the World In 8 Days*)

Navy commander and fighter ace Bill Hardy took off from his carrier in South Pacific WWII and saw a Japanese suicide plane coming for the carrier. He tested his guns, and it blew up, for which he saved many men and received the Navy Cross.

Personal Conversation with Pilot

The Japanese Zero fighter A6M5 lacked a sealed gas tank to protect the fuel tank from catching fire. US-Allied planes had them, but the Japanese did not until end of the war with A6M8. (Mikish, *Japanese Zero Fighter*)

Desert Storm began as US and five nations destroyed an enormous column of Russian tanks used by Iraqis. Saddam Hussein believed the tanks would work under cover of sandstorms, fog, and darkness. Our radars hunted them, and a variety of coalition aircraft destroyed them. An old Civil War axiom prevailed: "Get there the fastest with the mostest." (N. Schwarzkopf, autobiography of General Schwarzkopf)

Lieutenants Oakley Kelly and John Macready flew New York to California in 1923. First transcontinental US flight, which made it twenty-six hours, fifty minutes. Previous flights made them unable to fly over the mountains, and they had to pour soup into the engine to cool overheating. Plane is displayed on second floor of NMB.

When conducting blind tours, it is appropriate to take person's hand to feel front end of Airbus 321 nose to sense countersunk rivets designed to get more speed and allay drag. Personal tour recommendation.

Only one crew member flew on board both B-29s (*Enola Gay* and *Bock's Car*) in the atomic-bombing of Japanese cities Hiroshima and Nagasaki in 1945 WWII. Jacob Besor, from Baltimore, was the radar countermeasures officer. Planes normally carried twelve crew on these incredible missions. (P. Tibbets, *Enola Gay*)

A major principle of aviation is that the wing design must be asymmetrical—that is, a little flatter on the bottom and more roundish on upper surface. More air passes under the wing to buoy the aircraft up. The Wright brothers discovered this in their practical attempts to fly. (Lecture, J. Anderson)

The aircraft at right, flown on both sides of the Spanish Civil War, 1936–

1939, was the Nieuport Delage 52. Built in France, several found their way into combat in neighboring Spain. The Republicans had to face the same plane captured from the Nationalists when the war continued. (Internet sources)

Vin Fiz, an original Wright ex-model, was flown by Cal Rodgers from New York to California. It carried an advertisement for the grape drink. Historian E.P. Stein searched for one who had drunk it. His retort, "Vin Fiz tasted like river water." Rodgers made it to California after fifteen major crashes and significant injuries in forty-nine days. In April 1912, he crashed in the ocean and was killed. Only two original items exist on the plane: piece of the engine, or drip pan, and rudder, according to William Leaf's *Pilots' Directions*. His rebuilt plane is in the National Air and Space Museum.

General Jimmy Doolittle, hero of WWII, in his bombing of Tokyo, did much to improve the Army Air Corps throughout his career. He did much to save the reputation of the B-26, as it was called a "widow-maker" and other comments. He got crews together, jumped into *Marauder*, and made a few passes over the skeptical fliers in Florida. (Lowell Thomas, *Doolittle: A Biography*)

The Berlin Airlift was a Cold War situation in 1948–1949, and US planes flew from West Germany over Soviet-controlled East Germany to land in Berlin's Tempelhof Airport. Pilots had to land a fully loaded cargo plane like C-47 or C-54 onto a 5,600-foot airfield. If he did not make it, he was faced with a crash into a cemetery at the end of the runway. This was a deadly way to end a flight! (G. Halvorsen, *Candy Bomber*)

Captain Gail Halvorsen, the Berlin Airlift "candy bomber," on his first C-54 flight, did not encounter any problems. As the door of the plane opened, Berlin civilians, former WWII enemy soldiers, came out to unload the cargo. Halvorsen did not find any "supermen" or hateful veterans. They were grateful to Americans who came to Berlin to help them and orphans. (Halvorsen, *The Berlin Candy Bomber*)

In 1966, US tested the B-70a Valkyrie, and it had airborne collision with an F-104 fighter, killing Joe Walker, key test pilot, and another, Chris Cross, and a second crash saw US Air Force losing interest in the big superbombers.

Bombers can be replaced, but not test pilots. (R. Hallion, *Test Pilots*)

In Korean War, Communists had old Russian biplanes PO-2 that plagued the airports near the front. US Air Force moved some wrecked planes away from these targets and put up antiaircraft guns. When the PO-2s came back to drop their bombs, they were shot down. After some losses, the Communists never returned. (B. Aldrin, *Men from the Moon*)

Geraldine "Jerrie" Mock flew her Cessna 180 around the world in 1953, doing it a different way, from the Atlantic to North Africa. She flew alone and had many stays in peoples' homes. In the Middle East, authorities thought she was a man—not so—and got ovations. She donated her 180 to NASM in 1976, received a gold medal from President Johnson, and wrote her book *Three-Eight Charlie*.

First woman to fly was French, in 1910, Raymonde de la Roche, and she received a pilot's license. She flew to 15,700 feet and participated in the first airshow at Reims, France.

Captain Joe Kittinger, AF balloonist and pilot, flew balloon Manhigh I to a record-breaking altitude, to break a 1935 Army Air Service record of 72,400 feet by Anderson and Stevens. Kittinger continued upward and saw the blue skies turn to pitch-black as he was in space. He topped that by bailing out of a capsule at 102,800 feet, Excelsior III. His free fall was measured at 614 miles per hour, not quite Mach 1. Guinness World Records posted his parachute record.

Colonel Joe Kittinger next went into combat flying in the Vietnam War as an F-4 pilot. Besides his escapades, he has a humorous story of glass beer bottles. Pilots drink much, and the empty glasses pile up, so he got an idea to load up pickup trucks then place bottles in his aircraft. Next, he dropped the loads onto the Ho Chi Minh trail used constantly by the enemy at night. Many truck and bicycle tires were shredded by such glass. (Story from Kittinger's book *Come Up and Get Me*)

A giant of aviation industry, Bill Piper, bought out an

aircraft builder in the thirties for $400 and later sold the whole operation for $30 million and got his name in the Aviation Hall of Fame. His famed plane is the Piper Cub, which was helped along by US government subsidy for pilot licenses, called CPTP Civilian Pilots Training Program. A budding pilot could get thirty-two weeks of training and aircraft use free. (D. Francis, *Mr. Piper and His Cubs*)

PIPER "CUB"

Two Air Force pilots, Evans and Truman, flew a Cub around the world in 1947, which took four months and covered twenty-two thousand miles. Called the *Spirit of Washington*, it had an enhanced O-235 engine and now hangs in the Udvar-Hazy Museum in Chantilly, Virginia. (NASM Aviation in the Museum)

Sir Frank Whittle invented the jet engine, created the first patent for it, and paved the way for air transport to move faster. Many have said that he shrank the planet. During WWII, the 616 squadron was made up of Meteor jets in the RAF. Their assignment was to chase the German V-1 pulse jets, and they did by destroying at least nine. (J. Golley, *Whittle*)

The XA-15 Program, North American High-Altitude Research Program, began with Scott Crossfield as a test pilot and featured twelve men. A few became astronauts, like Neil Armstrong and Joe Engle, but Pete Knight achieved a world speed record of 4,520 miles per hour in 1967. MC-2 high-altitude pressure suit was the first successful pressure suit, according to J. Miller's *North American X-15: Aerofax Datagraph 2*.

First X-15 flight was with Scott Crossfield in 1959, Mach 2.11. On one flight smoke got into the cockpit with other problems. Crossfield was heard to say, "Holy smoke!" on an unrelated matter. (Hallion, *Test Pilot*)

Two atomic bombs were dropped to destroy two Japanese cities, Hiroshima and Nagasaki, and they resulted in Japan surrendering on battleship USS *Missouri* in September 1945. Little Boy, dropped on Hiroshima, weighed nine thousand pounds and had a twenty-eight-inch diameter, while Fat Man weighed ten thousand pounds. A teacher in my college was held to secrecy and could not tell anything that we asked. He worked on the tail fin of the bomb. (P. Tibbets, *Return of the* Enola Gay)

The fighter pilot who shoots down five enemy aircraft is an ace historically from the WWI French. They were championed by citizens, kids, and moviemakers. Baron Manfred von Richthofen, German ace, who downed 80 planes, was the king of the sky for his time. On to WWII to Korea and other brushfire wars, the top ace was German Erich Hartman with 352 "kills." Key problem was verification or so-called confirmation. Gun cameras installed in wing roots were essential, but in WWI, a pilot needed help from his ground forces. Some countries required ten enemy victories, or as Soviets had to sort out, "group kills." Still others, like Communist countries, did not accurately report losses and the like. (M. Spick, *Complete Fighter Ace*, and H. Seidl, *Stalin's Eagles*)

Top-notch enemy jet fighter in Korea was the Russian Mig-15, which sported good gun platform but was out-pointed by the US F86 Sabrejet. Sabre had a 10:1 kill ratio and was flown by superior pilots. Russians were surprise pilots but had inferior jet, though Yevgeni Papeleyev shot down thirty-three Allied planes in this type of craft. (Pepelaev, *Memoirs: MiG vs. Sabre,* in Russian)

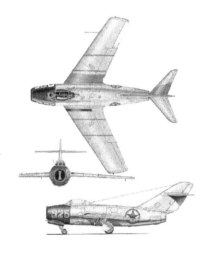

Navy lieutenant Everett Alvarez flew off US carrier *Constellation* in 1964 and was shot down over North Vietnam in 1964. He endured 8 1/2 years of captivity and torture and returned to duty. He wrote a book to describe the ordeal, received medals, and worked in the government. Following him was a long list of airmen who spent years in Communist prisons. In his book, he remarked that he would return to flying, but not on a carrier. (E. Alvarez, *Chained Eagle*)

A P-51 Mustang was shot up badly on a mission to Kiel, Germany, in 1943. The pilot tried to make the English Coast but fell into the English Channel. He radioed that it was a cold day to take a swim. Our rescue service never found him. We learned that the Mustang was a great aircraft but would not float very long in the water. (R. Grinsell, *P-51 Mustang*)

26
I 51-23 642-14 78343 Cross of Assos, flown by Colonel Olson P Burson, Officer Commanding 362nd Fighter Group. April 1945.

Meat shortage in UK during WWII had one crew receiving orders to fly B-17 with officers to Tunis after US forces landed in 1943. The plane flew an arc pattern to avoid Vichy, France (Nazi area with antiaircraft guns). Tunis was plentiful with wild horses, donkeys, and zebras. Crew loaded up with horse on oxygen and flew back to base. Bomb group had good meat then. Other flights were made, but on one, eastern winds blew a B-17 over the AA gun range and shot up the plane and killed a donkey with bloody mess inside. Crew dropped the dead animal over a Nazi-held town. (Conversation with WWII pilot)

First successful military jet to fly in US service was Kelly Johnson's P-80 (P for *Pursuit*) just before WWII ended. The "bugs" were discovered by courageous test pilots like Milo Burcham and Tony LeVier and others. It was sent abroad to protect our allies and flew in the Korean War. Nicknamed *LuluBelle*, it rests in the Smithsonian Museum. (T. LeVier, *Pilot*)

The late Chuck Yeager gave Jackie Cochran a tribute in her book when he described flying a Sabrejet to fifty thousand feet and a vertical dive past the sonic barrier wingtip to wingtip. Yeager said she made the world a safer and better place in which to live. (J. Cochran, *The Stars at Noon*)

The End

Here Are Some Personal Pictures for Use on the Cover

NATIONAL AIR & SPACE MUSEUM

Inside the text, with astronaut Tom Jones

The Mercury Seven

Next to the Apollo 11 command module

As a docent, you meet a lot of friends

Author's two thousandth tour with fourth
graders from a Virginia school

With Colonel Gail Halvorsen, "Candy Bomber"

Author with astronaut Victor Glover

With another school group from DC

About the Author

Bob Kovalchik has worked twenty-seven years as a volunteer docent (guide) and logged 2,087 tours. Most were general highlights, but many were VIP, space, school, and handicap tours for the blind and infirm. His career began as a secondary school teacher in Maryland until his retirement in 1991. He was also a travel consultant for groups in Europe, Russia, and China.

His writings include chapters for a book, *Europe Experience: Government and Culture*, as well as articles for Maryland Teacher and NASM docent monographs.